Terms and Conditions

LEGAL NOTICE

The Publisher has strived to be as accurate and complete as possible in the creation of this report, notwithstanding the fact that he does not warrant or represent at any time that the contents within are accurate due to the rapidly changing nature of the Internet.

While all attempts have been made to verify information provided in this publication, the Publisher assumes no responsibility for errors, omissions, or contrary interpretation of the subject matter herein. Any perceived slights of specific persons, peoples, or organizations are unintentional.

In practical advice books, like anything else in life, there are no guarantees of income made. Readers are cautioned to reply on their own judgment about their individual circumstances to act accordingly.

This book is not intended for use as a source of legal, business, accounting or financial advice. All readers are advised to seek services of competent professionals in legal, business, accounting and finance fields.

You are encouraged to print this book for easy reading.

Table Of Contents

Foreword

Chapter 1:
Introduction

Chapter 2:
The Basics of Marketing

Chapter 3:
Types of Advertising

Chapter 4:
The Soft Skills in Advertising

Chapter 5:
The Hard Skills You Will Need In Advertising

Chapter 6:
Principles In Writing a Marketing Ad

Chapter 7:
The Characteristics of the Best Advertising For Marketing.

Chapter 8:
The Benefits of Writing Killer Marketing Ads

Wrapping Up:
A-Z of Marketing Ads; Tricks and Tips.

Foreword

We are living in fast generation where everything gets changed within a minute. Advertising is a form of communication to promote the goods and services for sale. It is one of the parts of marketing. Advertising is a vast term and it includes many activities for the promotion of goods and services. Every company is trying to convince customers to buy their products and services. Get all the info you need here.

The Quintessential Guide to Marketing Ads
Everything You Need To Know To Survive In Advertising

Chapter 1:
Introduction

Synopsis

There is a very tough competition in the market for every product and services; therefore, every company has a separate department of advertising.

Advertising is a part of marketing and marketing departments invest a lot of money for advertising to increase the sales of the company.

Advertising is a way to connect to customers and public. Customers come to know about the products and services of different companies through advertising.

Advertising plays a very vital role in promoting goods and services. Advertising is a way of sending a message to the public; it portrays your organization, your products, values and services.

The Basics

Marketing is a wide term in promotion of goods and services. Marketing simply means "Giving the right product in the right place, at the right price, at the right time". Marketing is not only the promotion of goods and services, but it consists of knowing the needs of customers and then manufacturing the goods based on the customer demands, finding a place for promotion and distributing and transporting the goods to the required places. That is why we are saying Marketing is a very big term and advertising is a part of marketing.

Professor E. Jerome McCarthy has suggested the concept of marketing mix in 1960. Marketing mix is the key concept of advertising. Marketing mix consists of four "P" elements. Marketing mix includes the plans and ideas to bring the product into the market. Marketing mix consists of four elements: Product, Price, Place, Promotion. Now we discuss four elements:-

Product: - This product element refers to the product to be manufactured. It is very important to know about the customer needs and demands in the product. The company has to know the requirements of customer in product size, color and quality. After knowing all the requirements of customers, the company starts developing the product as per the customer demand.

Price: - Price is the money paid by the consumer for the product. The company needs to fix the price of the product after knowing the competitor's product prices and how much discount they can offer to attract the customers for goods and services.

Place: - Place refers to location to sell the products and services. The company has to find the place to market the products and services. Location should be easily reachable to customers and it should not be far from the customers. The market can be of different types, for example a physical market and or a virtual market. A physical market is where a customer interacts with the seller physically and buys the products as per the requirement. Virtual markets are those markets where buyers buy the product online and they do not meet physically.

Promotion: This is the last element of the marketing mix. Promotion means branding of products and services. Promotion means strategies and plans for advertisement of product, so that the product reaches the masses. It is awareness among the public regarding the product.

Chapter 2:
The Basics of Marketing

Synopsis

Marketing is a very old term in the business but used by different names. In the 18Th century, trade was the transfer of goods from one person to another person in exchange of goods. There has been a barter system where one person gives the goods in exchange for other goods. In simple meaning, we can say Exchange of surplus goods for the shortage goods. The reasons for surplus goods can be geographical location, skill labor and amount of labor etc and it can be the reason for shortage of particular goods.

Everyone has started to increase the production of goods and as the production of goods increases, limits and range of trade increased and so the distance between the traders. Because of this, it became difficult for every trader to locate other traders for business and exchange of goods. Then middlemen and intermediaries came into existence and their motive was to locate the trader and producer. So the middlemen's role was to bring together the two parties for business and this middlemen performed a lot of other roles and middlemen became a marketing department of the company.

What's It About

As defined by American Marketing Association, marketing is the business activities directed towards the flow of goods and services from the producer to the end user. It is an accumulation of all operations of business. Marketing is the mixture of all physical activities such as production, transportation, storage, distribution, promotion. Marketing is a very important component for success of any business. Marketing is the backbone of the organization and that is why companies are investing a lot of money in marketing.

Marketing is the creation and maintenance of relationship between company and the customers. Marketing is the not only important for the company but also it is important for the customers because customers come to know about the products and services through the marketing.

If the company does not do the marketing of products and services then how will customers come to know about the market of distribution of products and services? Therefore, marketing is vital component for the company and for the customers also.

Marketing's main motive is to get to know about the needs of customers and based on needs of customers, companies start the production and then promotion and distribution of goods and services. We can say it is planning, production, promotion and distribution of goods and services. If customers find the product at the right place, at right time and at right price than companies will make profits and it will be win-win situation for the company and for customers.

The success of marketing depends on the ability to communicate well with customers. Marketing needs effective planning, coordination of activities, directing of activities and review of operations. Marketing concepts hold the key to achieving the organizational goals, consisting of determining the needs and wants of the target customers and delivering the desired results more efficiently and effectively than competitors.

Under marketing concept, focus is on the selling satisfaction instead of selling the product. The objective of marketing is not the maximization of sales volume, but profit with the satisfaction of customers. The customer is the main point and all marketing activities work around the customer's satisfaction. It is essential for the entrepreneur to identify the customer's needs and deliver the goods and services as per the customer requirement.

Marketing begins with customer and ends with the customer. Since marketing is consumer oriented, it has a positive impact on the business firms. It enables the entrepreneurs to improve the quality of their goods and services.

Marketing helps in improving the standard of living of the people by offering a wide variety of goods and services with freedom of choice, and by treating the customer as the most important person. Marketing generates employment both in production and in distribution areas. Since a business firm generates revenue and earns profits by carrying out marketing functions, it will engage in exploiting more and more economic resources of the country to earn more profits.

A large-scale business can have its own formal marketing network, media campaigns, and sales force, but a small unit may have to depend totally on personal efforts and resources, making it informal and flexible. Marketing makes or breaks a small enterprise. An enterprise grows, stagnates, or perishes with the success or failure, as the case may be, of marketing.

Chapter 3:
Types of Advertising

Synopsis

As we have earlier discussed about the meaning of advertising, advertising is one of the methods of marketing to convince the customers to buy our products and services. It is one of the ways for promotion of goods and services.

Types

Advertising objectives largely determine the two basic types of advertising; product advertising and institutional advertising.

Product advertising is advertisement for selling the products and services. Its main aim is to sell the products to the end user.

Institutional advertising is advertisement for developing the goodwill of the company instead of selling the products. Its main objective is to improve the relation with other groups the company deals with.

Now there are many ways to advertise goods and services, so now we will discuss the ways through which we can advertise goods and services.
Advertising can be of different types:-

1) **Print Advertising** = Print advertising is a very old type of advertising. Print advertising is the method to advertise the product and services through publishing advertisements in newspapers and magazines. Print advertising also includes advertising through brochures and flyers. It is a very effective method for promoting goods and services. Print advertising is less costly compared to other types of advertising. Cost of print advertising in the newspaper is dependent on the quantity of the space, page of publication, quality of paper. Therefore, cost varies as per the requirement of the customer.

2) **Broadcast Advertising** = as per today's generation, broadcast advertising is very popular. Broadcast advertising means promotion of goods and services through television, radio and through online internet. Ads in television will cover a large audience and it is a very popular method of advertising. Advertisement on television is costly as compared to other advertisement because television advertisement covers a larger audience and is very much in demand. The radio advertising demand has come down because of television and internet advertising. Now the listeners of radio programs have come down, and because of this there is less demand for radio advertising. Internet advertising is the latest advertising method and very popular among the younger generation. Internet advertising consists of email marketing, social media marketing and Facebook marketing. Internet marketing also covers a large audience and is a very effective method to cover more audience for the products and services promotion.

3) **Outdoor Advertising** = Outdoor advertising uses different tools for customer attention. Outdoor advertising includes billboards, kiosks, events and tradeshows ways to promote the goods and services of companies. Billboards are available all over the country but the content should be attractive to induce the customers. Organizing the events and trade shows for promotion of goods and services is important. Events and trade shows are a very effective way to meet the customers directly

face to face. We can say outdoor advertising is very effective way for promotion and it is not very costly.

4) **Covert Advertising** = This is the latest trend of advertising and very unique. In this covert advertising in which a product or message is included in a TV serial or in a movie. This is not an actual ad in the TV. This is a very effective method of promotion and advertising. Suppose your favorite movie star uses a mobile phone of any company, then you will also want to use that company's mobile phone.

5) **Public service advertising** = This advertising is for the general awareness among the whole country or world, like AIDS awareness, Polio awareness, energy saving, Illiteracy, poverty and so on which need more awareness among the public.

Chapter 4:
The Soft Skills in Advertising

Synopsis

Communication is a very important component of any organization. Every company searches for employees who have good communication skills. Communication plays a vital role in every field and every organization. Person with good communication skills can be hire in any organization.

In today's world soft skills has become very important in every company. Soft skills play very important role in day-to-day operations. Soft skills are very important in every company and industry. Soft skills develop the interpersonal relations with the customers and clients. If you want to be successful in the advertising industry than you should have the good interpersonal skills with soft skills. Companies have soft skills trainer for improving the soft skills of their employees.

Employment experts say that you can get the interview call through the technical skills, but soft skills is what will actually get you the job and help you keep it.

Soft skill is a very broad term, but it includes the following concepts:-

1) **Communication** = Communication skills are a very important part of soft skills. The ability to communicate through spoken and written language is a need in every industry. Communication skill can be learned and improved through trainings. For example public speaking can be developed in trainings and it is a great confidence builder.

2) **Team Work** = The ability to work within a team is another soft skill and in today's world everybody should have the ability to work in a team. Organization consists of different departments and you should have good interpersonal skills to interact with your employees and with other departments. Companies are conducting team-building exercises for improving teamwork.

3) **Decision Making and Problem Solving** = Quick decision-making is one of the soft skills that every employee should have, especially the top management. Employees with problem solving abilities always get promotions to higher management.

4) **Adaptability** = To succeed in an organization, people should have passion to learn new things and work according to company requirements. People should learn new skills to adapt with the changing environment of the organization.

Chapter 5:
The Hard Skills You Will Need In Advertising

Synopsis

Hard skills are defined as the technical skills required for advertising. Hard skills simply mean the process and procedural knowledge of advertising. Hard skills are very important for every organization and for every field. If you have knowledge about advertising and promotion than only you are able to promote the goods and services for the companies. If the person does not have the knowledge of planning or organizing then how can the person conduct the marketing for the organization? In any career path, you should have the knowledge of a particular field. For example, if you want to become the doctor then you should have the knowledge to diagnose the illness or treat of any ailment.

Hard skills and soft skills shouldn't compete with each other, they should complement each other. Hard skills and soft skills need to be learned and developed to be successful in life.

The hard skills required for advertising are as follows:-

1) **Sales Skills** = You should have the knowledge about marketing and sales. You should have the capability to do the sales for the company and for that, you should have the knowledge about the product or service. You should have deep knowledge about the product, so that only you are able to explain the product or service to the end user.

2) **Analytical Skills** = You should have the capability to do analysis of the product and service of the organization. If you have the ability to do analysis, than you can easily come to know how to increase sales and how to promote the product and service to a large audience.

3) **Time Management** = A person should have knowledge about time management in order to be successful in advertising. Time management means scheduling the activities and completion of activities within the timeline.

4) **Product knowledge** = Product knowledge is very important for any advertising. Experts should have the deep knowledge about the products and services and should be able to explain them to a larger audience. In a democratic country, everybody has the right to question, so you should have the capability to explain the products and services.

5) **Creativity** = You should have the skills of creativity to think outside the box for attracting the customers. This is the unique part of advertising and every advertisement should be more compelling and different from the others. It should be more customer focused.

Chapter 6:
Principles In Writing A Marketing Ad

Synopsis

Writing a marketing Ad is difficult but not impossible. If you want to write an effective and persuasive Ad then you should follow some principles in writing good Ads.

Principles

1) **Honesty is the best policy** = While writing the Ad we should not hide any important thing from the customers. We should be open and give correct information to customers and it will definitely attract the customers. If the company is honest, people are more likely to stick with your products and services.

2) **AIDA Formula** = If you want your ad read by the mass audience, than you should make the ad more attractive and effective. Every company uses AIDA (Attention, Interest, Desire, Action) formula for attracting the customers. If you are not able to explain the product and service in an effective way or in interesting way than it will not be successful advertising. Therefore, we should add something attractive or offer something new, which attracts the customers and piques their interest and desire for the product and service.

3) **Attractive Headline** = The headline of the Ad should be big, easy to read and understand. It should tell you about the product and its advantages. The headline of the ad should tell you everything about the product and its benefits.

4) **Grasping your reader with pictures** = While writing marketing Ads, you should add pictures related to products and services. Pictures convey products and services well. Customers

are attracted by pictures instead of text. When we include pictures we should take proper care while adding pictures. Pictures should reflect products and services.

5) **Remove the risk** = Marketing ads should add the satisfaction guarantee and we should include the word warranty as well as the contact information in case the customers have any concerns or problems. Customers should think that buying the product will be a hassle free experience.

6) **Ads should have a compelling offer** = Advertisements should be effective and attractive to convince a large audience. Advertisements should be compelling because they will attract more customers and will be more compelling than the competitor's offer.

7) **Create a sense of urgency** = Advertisements should have a sense of urgency. They should show the benefits and needs of customers. Then customers will buy the products on an urgent basis. Customers always prefer to satisfy their needs, so companies should make advertisements that show a sense of urgency in regards to the product.

Chapter 7:
The Characteristics of the Best Advertisement for Marketing

Synopsis

Advertising employs different techniques to be successful. Advertising requires a lot of planning, organizing, directing and coordination of activities to be successful. Marketing research is very important for successfully running a business.

Marketing research is the first step for making the best advertisement. It helps an entrepreneur to make decisions concerning the type of product, the price policy, the channel of distribution, and sales promotion can be made correctly with the help of marketing information at the right time. It is the gathering, recording, and analysis of all facts about problems relating to the transfer and sale of goods and services from producer to consumer.

For example, a hotel should find out what services are needed to satisfy its customers and the soft toy manufacturer making teddy bears needs to find out if children really want purple teddy bears and so on.

What's Best

Every company, regardless of size, must research its market, customers and competition initially to set it on the right course and then continually to monitor its performance. Small-scale firms are often unable to afford continuous marketing research. However, they can use personal contacts and other informal methods for collecting required information about markets. Marketing information can be collected from the primary sources and secondary sources. Primary sources consist of customers, dealers, salesman, and secondary sources, such as newspapers, magazines, and publications of financial institutions.

Your ads should have the capability of generating interest in larger audiences for your products and services. If your ads are not able to attract the customers, then we should check the points where we are lacking. The following are the characteristics of the best advertisements;-

1) **Zero in on your best** prospects = Many business owners make the mistake of thinking bigger is better and spending a lot of money on advertising. They do not focus on their market. For example if your company provides help to law firms in solving cases and you are giving full page advertisements in the New York Times instead of the New York Law Journal, you will definitely get the disappointed response from the advertisement campaign. You should be focused and advertise the product and service where there is a need of your services.

2) **Set Yourself Apart from the Crowd** = Your advertisement should be unique and different from the competitors to attract the customers and large audiences. Unless your business sells unique goods and services and faces no competition, your ads should be unique and different from the competitors.

3) **Demonstrate Value** = Your advertisement should be effective and different from the competitors so you can demonstrate the value of your products and services. You should explain the benefits of your products and services and how they are different from your competitor's products and services. For example, you can give different offers and benefits with your products and services.

4) **Focus on client problems** = Customers buy products to solve their problems and fill their needs. Therefore, you need to focus on customers' needs and their problems. You should be more focused on client's problems in your advertisements, if you want to attract the customers.

5) **Require Action** = The final action of an effective ad is a call to action. If you have completed the job of advertisement until this point, and your prospect did not call for products, then you should take action, and instruct them to call you for help and service.

Chapter 8:

The Benefits of Writing Killer Marketing ads

Synopsis

If you want to be successful in the business then you need a loyal customer base for your products and services. Even if your company provides high quality products and services at a reasonable price, if customers do not have the knowledge of your products and services then you are not able to make the sales.

The best marketing ads help the business to grow and attract more customers day by day. That's why companies are investing millions of dollars in advertising because companies know that they will earn double if they are able to attract the customers in larger prospect.

Now we will discuss the benefits of writing a killer marketing ad and how best marketing ads will help the business to grow.

The Benefits

1) **Attracting Customers** = One of the benefits of killer marketing ads is that it can attract new customers and audiences. New customers will come to know the products and services and it will increase the sale for the company. Loyal customers are more powerful because they tell others about goods and services.

2) **Improving Sales Figures** = The end goal of every advertisement is to increase the sales and if you have good marketing ads, you will definitely attract more customers and increase the sales of the company. Increases in sales will cover the cost of advertisements also. Improvements in sales will improve the finance structure of the company and the company can expand with good finances.

3) **Attracting Investors** = A company with high profits and a large customer base will definitely attract investors to invest in your company. That is the benefit of writing killer marketing ads because it not only attracts the customers but also it attracts the private investors for investing in your business.

4) **Competition** = If you have good marketing for your products and services, it will be tough competition to your competitors. It will not increase profits but it will decrease the confidence of your competitors. Therefore, there is a need for good writing in

ads because then we will attract larger audiences and it will increase the sales of the company.

5) **Brand Name** = Writing a killer ad will not only attract the customers but it will make a brand name in the national and international market. Everybody will come to know about the company logo and products. Brand name is very important for the goodwill of the company. If you have goodwill than investors will invest in your company.

6) **Finance** = There are many benefits of good advertising. As it will attract more customers and it will increase the sales and side-by-side, it will make a brand name in the market. Suppose if a company wants to expand their business, you need a loan from the financial institution. You will get the loans easily because of your brand name.

Wrapping Up
A-Z of Marketing Ads; Tricks And Tips.

Marketing is a wide term and before we start the marketing planning, a company should have the knowledge about the market for selling products and services.

A market consists of a large number of individual customers who differ in terms of their needs, preferences and buying capacity. Therefore, it becomes necessary to divide the total market into different segments or homogeneous customer groups. Such division is called market segmentation. They may have uniformity in employment patterns, educational qualifications, economic status, preferences, etc.

Market segmentation enables the entrepreneur to match his marketing efforts to the requirements of the target market. Instead of wasting his efforts in trying to sell to all types of customers, a small-scale unit can focus its efforts on the segment most appropriate to its market.

Every company is working hard in advertising to attract more customers and to increase the sales figure. That is why companies are investing a lot in advertising because some of the advertising is a one time fixed investment, if you get more customers in one advertisement.

Advertising is a part of marketing and marketing is a very big term and now we will discuss marketing, advertising ideas, tips and tricks to attract more customers and have deep knowledge about the marketing and advertising. Following are the guidelines and tips of marketing and advertising.

1) **Know your customers** = You should have the knowledge about your customer base. You should know the types of customers you will attract. Why should customers buy your product? If you have knowledge about your customers then you are able to do marketing in an effective way and attract customers who need your products and services.

2) **Create a Survey** = Every company is doing a survey related to their products and services. A survey tells you about the customer's needs and demands. Information gathered from the survey will be very beneficial for marketing. Marketing department will forward this information to production department for producing the goods as per the customer demands.

3) **Use Deadlines** = If a company is giving a discount or offer on any product and services then it should have the deadline.

There should be a time lime for the offer because customers will hurry to buy your products and services.

4) **Examine promotional materials** = Whatever the promotional materials used for promotion are, it should be checked. Companies should examine the promotional materials like business cards, letterheads, brochures, flyers and other packaging material. There should be no spelling mistakes in any promotional items.

5) **Magic Words-"Thank You"** = Companies should send letters to their loyal customers for purchasing the goods and services. Thank you is the magic word and always works on the customers. Companies can say thank you through letters, phone calls or by email also.

6) **Secrets of marketing** = First you must be consistent in advertising. So advertising should be consistent because your customers will forget you if they do not hear from you. You must be confident about the results of your advertisement. Sometime advertisement takes time to produce results. Therefore, you should have patience.

7) **Never Assume** = While making any advertisement, never assume the following things, like that the customers cannot afford it, the customers won't buy it, the customers doesn't

understand the product, or the customer won't be able to pay the price of the product.

8) **Knowledge about the demographics of your sales area** = Companies should collect the information about the sales area. We should have the knowledge about the local newspaper and their advertising prices, local TV and radio stations because they will easily attract the local public.

9) **Competitors offers** = You should be up to date with the competitors offering your products and services. If you have the knowledge about the competitor's promotion and offerings, you can easily make your marketing more effective.

10) **Seminar and Events** = Companies should do the seminar and events for the promotion of goods and services. This is the best idea to have direct interaction with the customers. You should be an expert in your products and services and be able to answer the customer's queries. Seminars help cement relations with current customers, attract prospects, and increase your company's exposure.

11) **Social Media Advertising** = Social media marketing has taken over the marketing industry nowadays and reason for it is the number of advantages that an individual gets. If an organization or industry promotes its product through the social networking sites, they connect to the masses very easily

and it gives them a better chance to reach people as they get to know more about the company updates. Every sector today makes use of this social media for promoting its product whether it is a cosmetology industry or the movies or the various clothes brands. Every company has a website to promote their goods and services. Websites are the best way to tell about offers and promotional events.

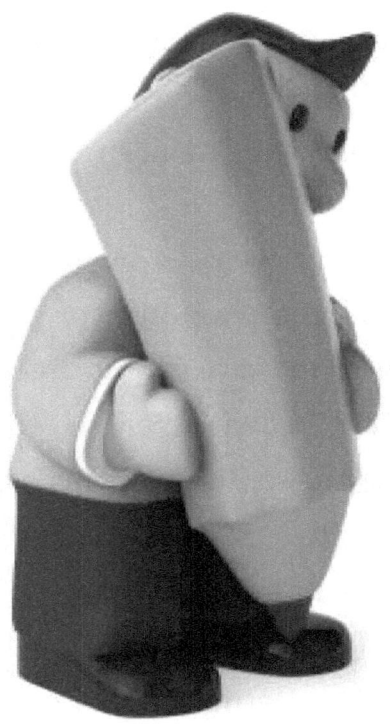

www.ingramcontent.com/pod-product-compliance
Lightning Source LLC
Chambersburg PA
CBHW030549220526
45463CB00007B/3038